A VISUAL GUIDE TO THE
FLA
OF THE
WORLD

V S de Kleer

CHATHAM PUBLISHING
LONDON

Copyright © V S de Kleer 2005

First published in Great Britain in 2007 by
Chatham Publishing
Lionel Leventhal Ltd,
Park House, 1 Russell Gardens,
London NW11 9NN

Distributed in the United States of America by
MBI Publishing Company
Galtier Plaza, Suite 200, 380 Jackson Street,
St Paul, MN 55101-3885, USA

First published in 2005 in Canada by Nimbus Publishing Ltd

British Library Cataloguing in Publication Data

De Kleer, Vicki
Flags of the world : a visual guide
1. Flags
I. Title
929.9'2

ISBN-13: 9781861763051

Library of Congress Cataloging-in Publication Data available

Printed and bound in Hong Kong through Printworks Int. Ltd.

Dedicated to the officers and crew of the
Sail Training Ship Lord Nelson.

The STS *Lord Nelson* enables men and women with disabilities to crew this ship efficiently during any voyage, long or short. Built in 1985, designed by noted naval architect Colin Mudie, and named after Britain's premier handicapped sailor, the *Lord Nelson* has proven to be a highly effective vessel. From its homeport of Southampton, this 170-foot barque sails the coasts of Europe as well as the north Atlantic Ocean.

Acknowledgements

TWO STEPS WERE vital to the inception of this book: inspiration and encouragement. The first step was joining the STS *Lord Nelson* in time for the Tall Ships Challenge in Halifax in August 2000. There were more flags in the harbour than anyone could count. This wonderful sight inspired me to develop a way to sort them out!

Just as important was the encouragement I received to rearrange the flags into book form for easy identification. This came from Bishop D. R. Spence, past president of the North American Vexillological Society and a Fellow of the Royal Heraldry Society of Canada.

Thanks also to many other people who contributed constructive ideas and their own expertise, among them:

Brian Dexter and Cathy Hunt for photographs; Halton Camera Exchange, Georgetown, Ontario for such prompt photographic work; Kennedy's Specialty Sewing Limited, Erin, Ontario; Dave Hunter, for book structure; Peter Edwards and Bishop D. R. Spence, both vexillologists; M. K. Zavitz, author profile; Halifax Citadel, National Historic Site of Canada; John Lang, The Cruise People, Toronto; Wing Commander T. E. Moszkowski; the aptly named Office Magic, Georgetown, Ontario; Captain R. J. Williams, Dream Maker Software; Dr. Whitney Smith, founder of the Flag Research Center in Massachusetts for proofreading; Rand McNally Canada Inc. for the maps; and, while all this was going on, constant support from my husband, George.

I particularly appreciate the expertise of Nimbus Publishing in bringing the original manuscript through all the complex stages of development to the final printed and bound volume.

Table of Contents

Preface

FOR MANY YEARS I have been interested in flags, where they come from, and what they mean. This interest led me to search through vexillological texts—where flags are invariably listed alphabetically, geographically, or even politically—until I would almost accidentally come across the one I wanted to identify. But flags are graphic, and we ought to be able to identify them by their visual pattern.

This became more obvious to me when hundreds of vessels—from small sloops to square-riggers—sailed into Halifax during the Tall Ships Challenge 2000. Halifax was the last port of call before the finish line in Amsterdam, and this was the largest fleet that had ever been in Halifax harbour. Ships representing twenty-five countries from around the world were "dressed overall" for the festivities, which meant there were numerous ensigns and hundreds of signal flags flying. It was then, faced with an overwhelming collection of flags on a multitude of masts, that I had the idea for an identification system organized by graphic elements.

There are certainly well-illustrated books available to those who want to find out more about a given flag, but they are not grouped by design or colour. The human eye and brain have the built-in ability to recognize the language of patterns and shades, and can match shapes and colours almost instantly. This field guide takes advantage of this skill.

The benefit of this book is the quick identification of flags. It is but an introduction to vexillology; once you have discovered where a flag comes from, you can consult many other texts for further information on the flag or its country of origin.

The World

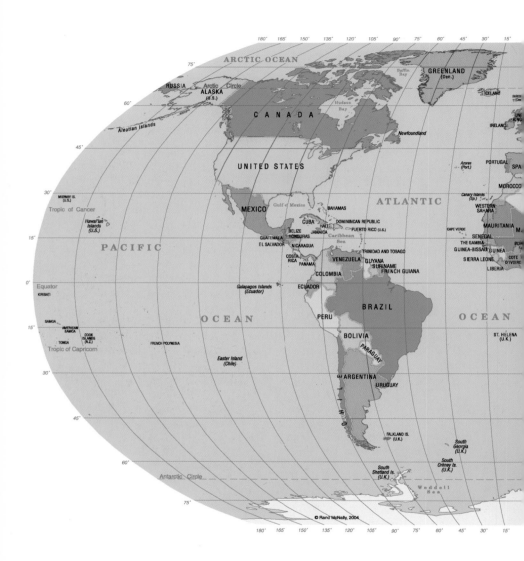

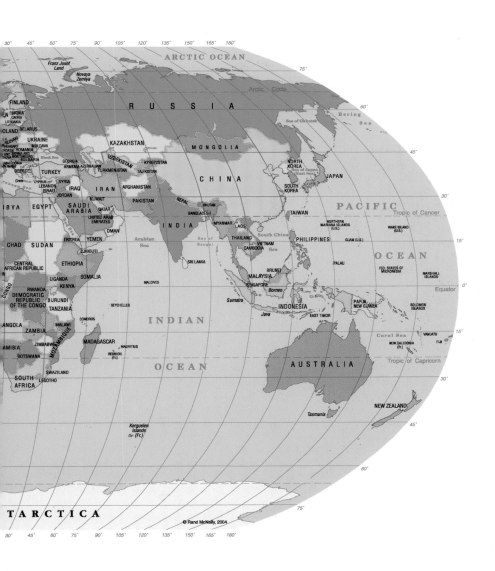

The Anatomy of a Flag

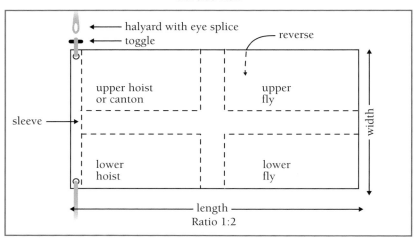

Dura-lite Co. U.S.A.
95% Nylon. 5% other fabric
12" x 18"

grommet   sleeve   Great Britain

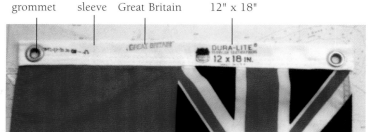

This UK Civil Ensign shows the data that may be supplied by the manufacturer.

Introduction

A Quick History of Flags

 FLAGS HAVE BEEN in use for at least five thousand years, from the times of ancient civilizations. They are designed with strong patterns and contrasting colours to announce the identity of territories, armies, ships, friends, or foes.

Flags must be easy to recognize at a distance by the unaided eye, and for that reason they have to be distinct, even striking, in appearance. A flag measuring three feet by six feet can be recognized from about two kilometres away with no magnification. The advent of telescopes and binoculars has markedly increased the distance over which flags can be read.

Although flags are now made of cloth, their earliest predecessors did not fly, but were carved from wood, often into subjects such as eagles and lions. Their main purpose was to identify the bearer, but they were also decorated so as to put fear into the hearts of opponents, and adorned with gifts to ensure victory. They were called **vexilloids**, and it is from this word that we derive the modern term **vexillology**, the study of flags.

Later, vexilloids were replaced by fabric flags that flew from a **staff** carried by foot soldiers or horsemen. Their prime purpose—to identify troops or armies—remained unchanged. Through time, particularly in the twelfth and thirteenth centuries, **banners** and **pennants** became quite magnificent. Their ornate and rich designs were closely associated with heraldry and therefore carried much meaning. Royal families, knights, and lords in Europe carried their own **standards** on peaceful occasions as well as during wartime. The fabric varied among silk, linen, wool, and cotton. Gold and silver metallic thread was frequently worked in, and many designs were carried out in beautiful detail.

Times change, and although **bunting**—a fine woven wool—is still sometimes used for high quality flags, natural fibres have largely been replaced by modern synthetic fabrics. These newer materials have many advantages: they are lightweight, dry quickly, and rot resistent. Such virtues are particularly important for flags used at sea.

Appliqué is the preferred method for constructing ceremonial and other special flags. Sewn by hand or by machine individually, the labour and skill involved in making these flags means that the cost is relatively high. Most flags, however, now have their designs silk-screened, stamped on, or otherwise applied by methods suitable for mass production.

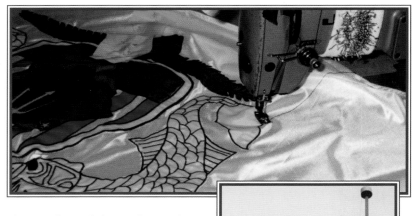

Flags can be made by machine or by hand, which affects both the cost and the final quality of the product.

Now that flags are produced by the thousands, they can be seen in profusion at sporting events, each fan waving the colours of a favourite team. The opening ceremonies of the Olympic Games, where national flags are paraded into the arena, is probably the best occasion to see the world's flags gathered together in a peaceful atmosphere.

As you watch for flags, you will notice that there is often a ceremony involved when one is raised or lowered. This is particularly true in a military context. Since a flag represents its country and citizens, it should always be treated with respect. It should never touch the ground, nor should one flown at sea be allowed to trail in the water. During a time of national or personal mourning, flags are flown at half-mast for a limited time, on land or aboard vessels in port. Each flag is raised all the way up its staff, then it is brought halfway down. Similarly, when the flag is to be lowered, it is raised all the way to the top and then brought down completely. The flags in the above illustration are at half-mast for the death of an officer, with the national flag above the police unit flag. They will stay in this position until the day after the funeral, when once again all flags will fly at the mast-head.

An effective way to **hoist** a flag is to fold it lengthwise, then roll it up tightly. The **halyard** is bent on as usual, but the **downhaul** component is then held around the flag with a slip knot. The flag is hoisted up with the downhaul just slack. Once in position, that is pulled down sharply, releasing the flag to fly freely. This looks impressive on a windy day as the flag appears to burst from the top of its pole.

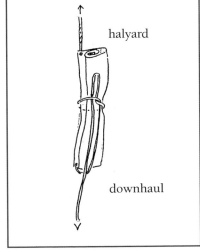

halyard

downhaul

It is a point of honour that a flag be in good condition, with its colours bright. A worn or faded flag should be repaired or replaced. An exception is flags that have been damaged in battle: shot through, scorched, or torn. Such a flag may be **retired**, or **laid up**, and hung in a place of honour. All other flags should be burnt, not tossed out casually.

It is evident from news coverage of international conflicts that one of the worst insults is to publicly set alight, stamp on, or otherwise desecrate and insult an enemy's flag. Another rule—frequently disregarded—is that flag designs should not be used out of their intended context—for instance, they should never appear on clothing or other items.

Seeing Double

Flag identification can be tricky! Look carefully at the flags below. Are they the same, or different?

On the left is a flag from Côte d'Ivoire, showing its obverse side, and the reverse image to its right. The Irish flag, on the right, happens to use the same colours and design in the opposite way. It would be easy to mistake one for the other if you did not take note of the position of the staff. Remember: flags are depicted to the right of their staves. Because there are only so many flag designs and colours that can be used, mistaking one flag for another can happen easily.

A Vexillological Puzzle

Test your ability to distinguish between flags of similar design and colour. There are at least sixteen flags in the below figure: can you find them all?(Colour tones and shapes may vary.)

(Answer on page 45)

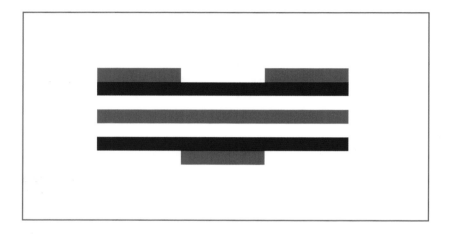

Using the Guide

Organizing Principles

The flags in this guide are arranged according to several key visual elements. These are explained below in the order by which they are applied, namely, design, colour, shape (ratio), and complexity.

1. Design

Flags are organized in this guide first with respect to basic design, which usually falls within common patterns, such as two horizontal bands, four vertical bands, a solid colour with a circle on it, diagonal lines, etcetera. These basic patterns are all depicted on pages 8 and 9, with corresponding page references to world flags of this type.

If the field has an additional design superimposed on it, the flag may be grouped either by background or by the defacement on it. **Defacements** may be stars, small crests, or other designs. Generally, such flags are categorized by the additional design elements unless the defacement is very small.

Also important are larger design elements, which are usually important to the flag as a whole. A good example is the red dragon on the flag of Wales (26-E-2). The dragon comes to notice immediately, so the Welsh flag is placed with other flags that display a heraldic creature.

2. Colour

The next organizing principle is that of colour. Once a flag has been grouped according to its basic design, it will be arranged on the page in the following order according to colour: red, white, yellow, blue, green, and black.

All flags with a red horizontal band on top will then appear at the top of the page, and a flag with a green and black colour scheme will likely appear at the bottom of the page.

If a flag has multiple colours, the first colour considered in sequence will be that of the design element by which it is first grouped. For example, flags on the page arranged by a horizontal cross design (see page 21) are ordered according to the colour of the cross, so red crosses appear first, and so on.

Flags arranged by prominent colours (see pages 27–29) are arranged slightly differently. These flags are also classed by how many colours appear in the flag. Therefore, on the page of prominently red flags (see page 27), the first flags are those with one colour, then two colours, then three, etcetera. The following three flags illustrate an example of this organizing principle.

B
(one colour)

Hong Kong
(two colours)

Wallis and Fortuna
(three colours)

3. Shape (Ratio)

Most flags in this book are rectangular, with a ratio of about 1:2 or longer. However, some flags are square or triangular. Shapes appear in this order: square, rectangle, triangle.

4. Complexity

In general, flags are organized from left to right according to increasing complexity of design. A flag with three horizontal stripes and a small central design is considered more complex than a flag with three plain horizontal stripes. For example, the Argentina civil flag (below left) is considered less complex than the Argentina national flag.

Argentina,
civil ensign

Argentina,
national

Also of Note:

Finally, flags that are considered equal with respect to their final organizing element will be arranged alphabetically. For example, two flags with the same colour scheme and degree of complexity will be placed in alphabetical order.

Some, but not all, flags are cross-referenced. Flags that have been cross-referenced generally correspond equally to two major design patterns. If you do not find a flag under one part of its design, look up another component.

You will find national flags and those of the International Code of Signals in this book, but you will come across many more specialized flags flying in the wind: pennants, elaborate banners, city and state flags. There will also be new flags as changing national politics across the world dictate.

An alphabetical index at the back of the book makes searching by country easy.

Using this Guide: A Summary

1 Determine the basic pattern of the unknown flag.
Is it made up of stripes? Are the bands vertical, diagonal, or horizontal?
Does it have a well-defined circle?
The basic flag designs on pages 8–9 will give you the range of designs
from which to choose.

2 Turn to pages 8-9.
Match your flag with the most similar basic design.

3 Keeping the organizing principles—not only design, but also colour,
shape, and complexity—in mind, scan the flags in search of one similar to
your unknown flag.

4 Compare your unknown flag with a known illustration and discover
which country it belongs to.

Example: You would like to identify this flag.

1 It has three horizontal bands, and the colour order is red, white, and
blue.

2 Turn to pages 8–9, and locate horizontal band designs.
Turn to pages 13–17, as instructed. Find three horizontal band designs,
which start on page 14.

3 The top band of the unknown flag is red, so start your search near the
top of page 14. Line C has two flags similar to the one you're looking
for—note the darker blue is the closest match to your flag.

4 Your previously unidentified flag is in position C-2 on page 14, the
national flag of The Netherlands.

Basic Flag Designs

Horizontal bands

2 bands / p. 13

3 bands / pp. 14-16

4+ bands / p. 17

Vertical bands

2 bands / p. 18

3+ bands /
pp. 19-20

Squares

squares / p. 20

grid / p. 20

Quartered with horizontal cross

p. 21

Triangle along one border

p. 22

Diagonal

multiple diagonal /
p. 23

Diagonal

single diagonal /
p. 23

Fan

p. 23

Union Flag incorporated

p. 24

Band on
hoist border

p. 25

Square or oblong on
upper hoist

p. 25

Circle or ring

p. 26

Heraldic creature

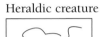

p. 26

Solid X

p. 26

X

p. 26

Diamond

p. 26

Field Colour

Red / p. 27

White / p. 28

Yellow / p. 28

Blue / p. 29

Green / p. 29

International Code of Signals:
Alphabet: pp. 30-33
Numerals: p. 34
Repeat Flags: p. 35
Code and Answer Pennant: p. 35

Try using these flags for practice.

As with all code signals, the set of five flags in the image to the left must be read from the top down. In this case, ignore the uppermost flag as it is the house flag of the shipping company.

(See p. 45 for answers.)

Flags

So MANY EVENTS are at the mercy of the wind.
Without the lightest trace of it flags are inscrutable.
We simply have to wait patiently for the arrival of
a breath, a breeze, a gale, or a storm
in order to read the language of flags.

Horizontal Bands (2)

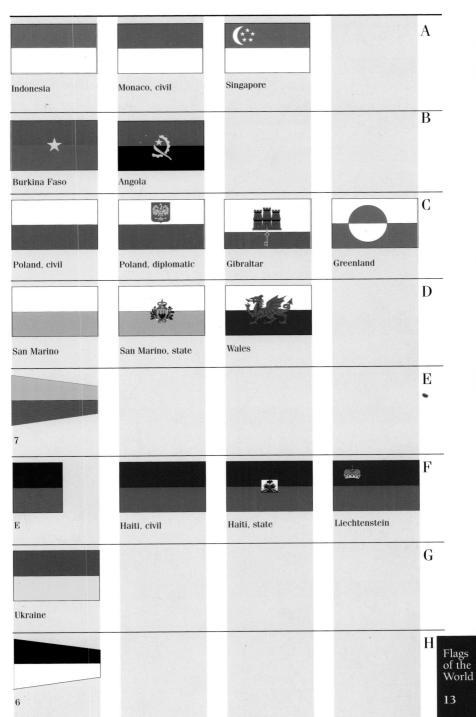

A

Indonesia   Monaco, civil   Singapore

B

Burkina Faso   Angola

C

Poland, civil   Poland, diplomatic   Gibraltar   Greenland

D

San Marino   San Marino, state   Wales

E

7

F

E   Haiti, civil   Haiti, state   Liechtenstein

G

Ukraine

H

6

1   2   3   4

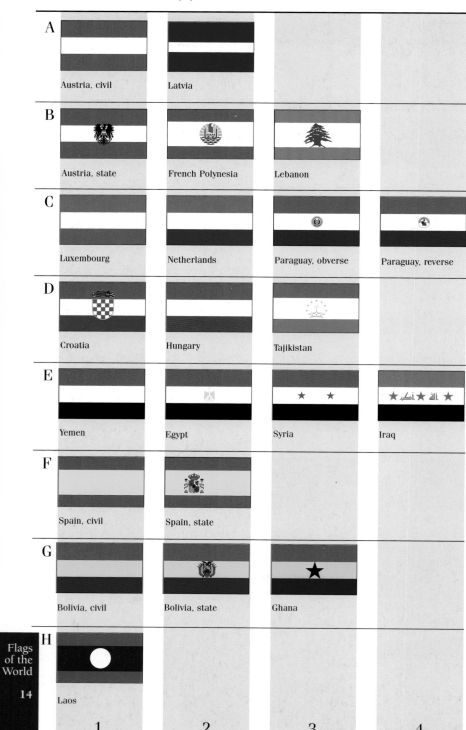

A — Austria, civil — Latvia

B — Austria, state — French Polynesia — Lebanon

C — Luxembourg — Netherlands — Paraguay, obverse — Paraguay, reverse

D — Croatia — Hungary — Tajikistan

E — Yemen — Egypt — Syria — Iraq

F — Spain, civil — Spain, state

G — Bolivia, civil — Bolivia, state — Ghana

H — Laos

1   2   3   4

Horizontal Bands (3)

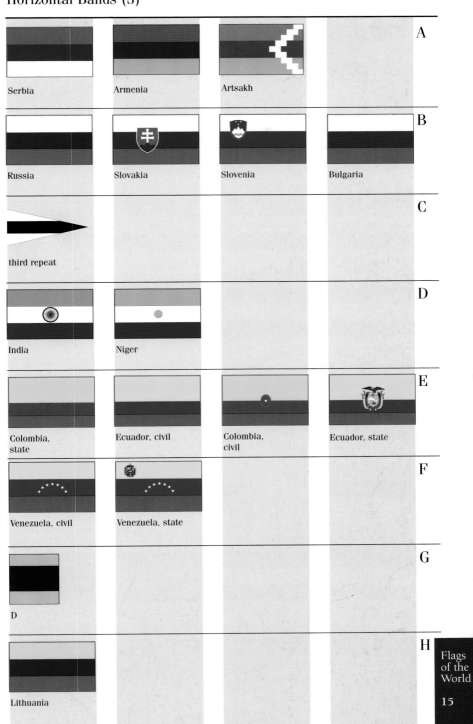

A

Serbia   Armenia   Artsakh

B

Russia   Slovakia   Slovenia   Bulgaria

C

third repeat

D

India   Niger

E

Colombia, state   Ecuador, civil   Colombia, civil   Ecuador, state

F

Venezuela, civil   Venezuela, state

G

D

H

Lithuania

1   2   3   4

Horizontal Bands (3)

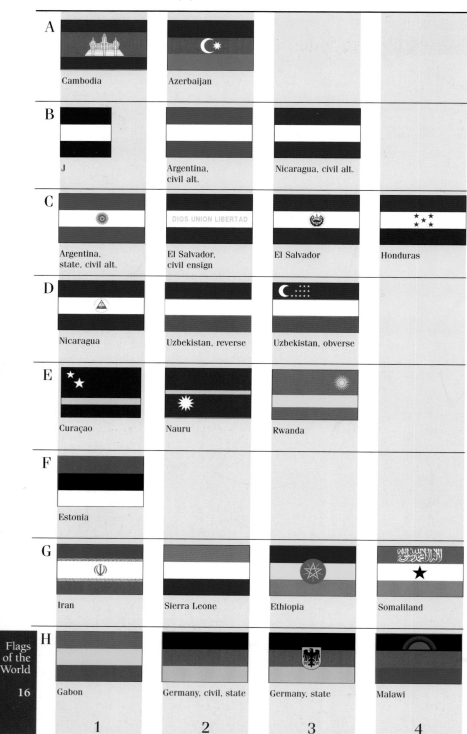

A Cambodia | Azerbaijan

B J | Argentina, civil alt. | Nicaragua, civil alt.

C Argentina, state, civil alt. | El Salvador, civil ensign — DIOS UNION LIBERTAD | El Salvador | Honduras

D Nicaragua | Uzbekistan, reverse | Uzbekistan, obverse

E Curaçao | Nauru | Rwanda

F Estonia

G Iran | Sierra Leone | Ethiopia | Somaliland

H Gabon | Germany, civil, state | Germany, state | Malawi

1   2   3   4

Horizontal Bands (4 or more)

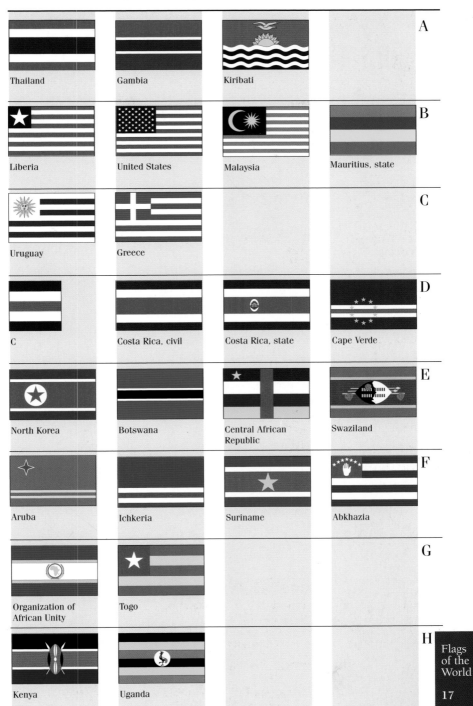

A

Thailand

Gambia

Kiribati

B

Liberia

United States

Malaysia

Mauritius, state

C

Uruguay

Greece

D

C

Costa Rica, civil

Costa Rica, state

Cape Verde

E

North Korea

Botswana

Central African Republic

Swaziland

F

Aruba

Ichkeria

Suriname

Abkhazia

G

Organization of African Unity

Togo

H

Kenya

Uganda

1

2

3

4

Vertical Bands (2)

A

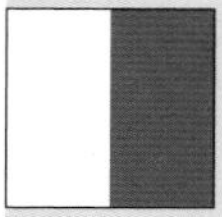

H

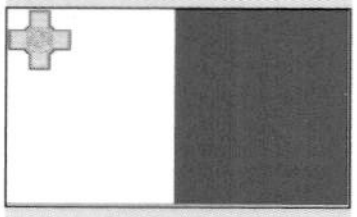

Malta

B

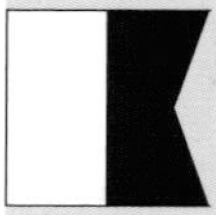

A

C

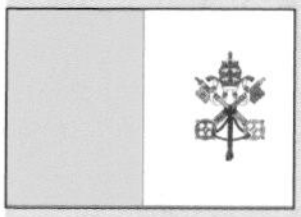

Vatican City

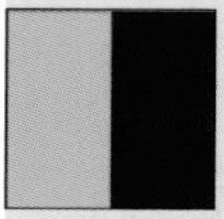

K

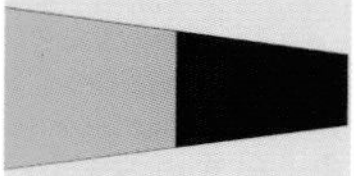

5

D

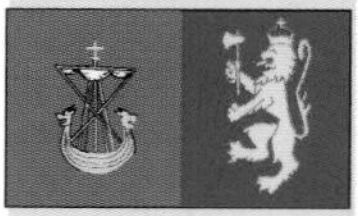

Orkney Islands

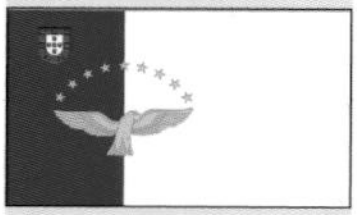

Azores

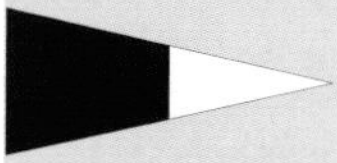

second repeat

E

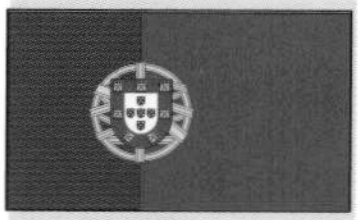

Portugal

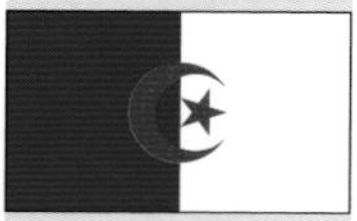

Algeria

1 2 3 4

Vertical Bands (3 or more)

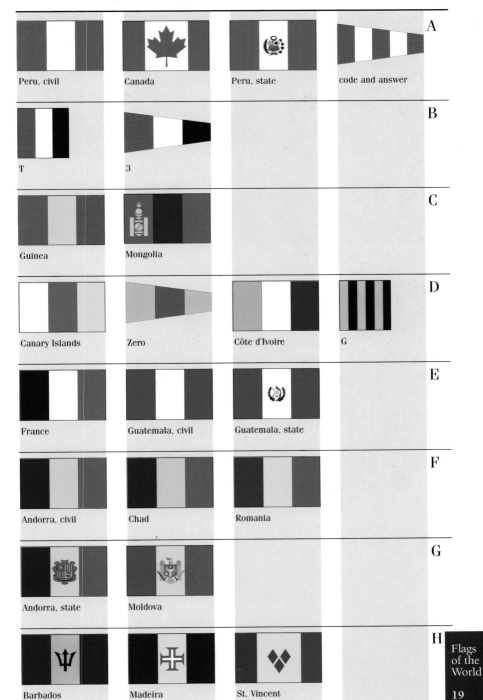

1	2	3	4
A Peru, civil	Canada	Peru, state	code and answer
B T	3		
C Guinea	Mongolia		
D Canary Islands	Zero	Côte d'Ivoire	G
E France	Guatemala, civil	Guatemala, state	
F Andorra, civil	Chad	Romania	
G Andorra, state	Moldova		
H Barbados	Madeira	St. Vincent	

Vertical Bands (3 or more)

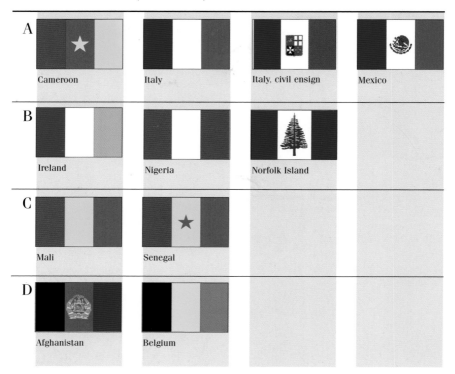

A
Cameroon
Italy
Italy, civil ensign
Mexico

B
Ireland
Nigeria
Norfolk Island

C
Mali
Senegal

D
Afghanistan
Belgium

Squares

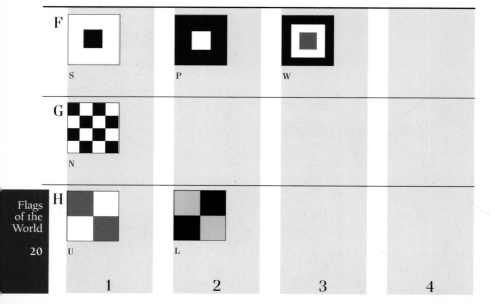

F
S
P
W

G
N

H
U
L

1   2   3   4

Quartered with Horizontal Cross

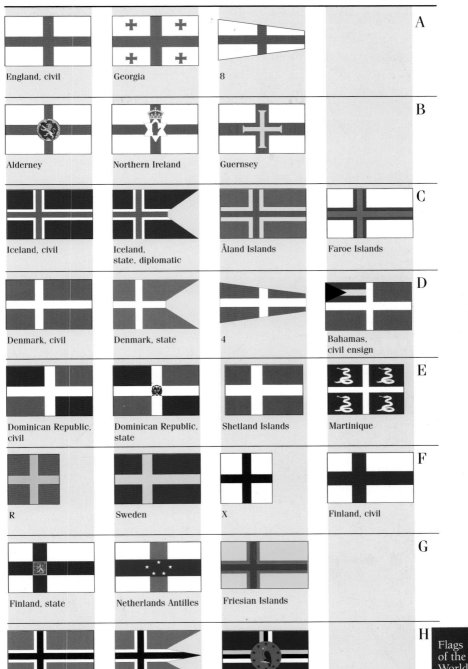

England, civil   Georgia   8   **A**

Alderney   Northern Ireland   Guernsey   **B**

Iceland, civil   Iceland, state, diplomatic   Åland Islands   Faroe Islands   **C**

Denmark, civil   Denmark, state   4   Bahamas, civil ensign   **D**

Dominican Republic, civil   Dominican Republic, state   Shetland Islands   Martinique   **E**

R   Sweden   X   Finland, civil   **F**

Finland, state   Netherlands Antilles   Friesian Islands   **G**

Norway, civil   Norway, state   Dominica   **H**

1   2   3   4

Flags of the World

21

Triangle along One Border

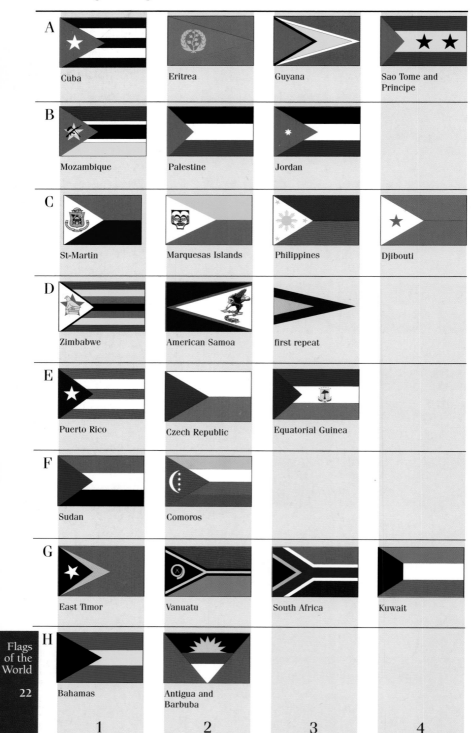

	1	2	3	4
A	Cuba	Eritrea	Guyana	Sao Tome and Principe
B	Mozambique	Palestine	Jordan	
C	St-Martin	Marquesas Islands	Philippines	Djibouti
D	Zimbabwe	American Samoa	first repeat	
E	Puerto Rico	Czech Republic	Equatorial Guinea	
F	Sudan	Comoros		
G	East Timor	Vanuatu	South Africa	Kuwait
H	Bahamas	Antigua and Barbuba		

Diagonal or Fan Design

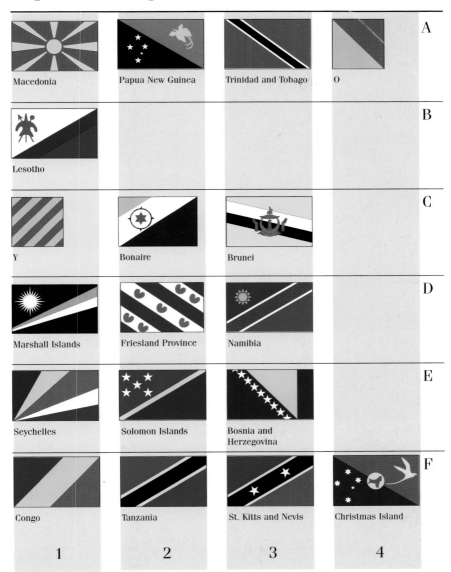

A

Macedonia

Papua New Guinea

Trinidad and Tobago

O

B

Lesotho

C

Y

Bonaire

Brunei

D

Marshall Islands

Friesland Province

Namibia

E

Seychelles

Solomon Islands

Bosnia and
Herzegovina

F

Congo

Tanzania

St. Kitts and Nevis

Christmas Island

1

2

3

4

Union Flag Incorporated

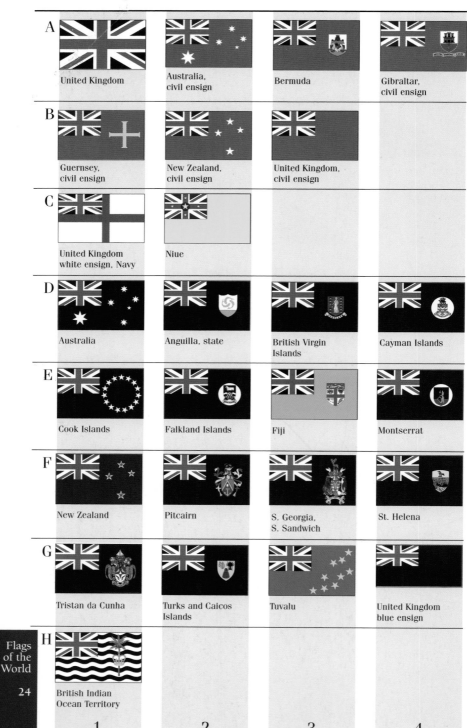

A
United Kingdom

Australia,
civil ensign

Bermuda

Gibraltar,
civil ensign

B
Guernsey,
civil ensign

New Zealand,
civil ensign

United Kingdom,
civil ensign

C
United Kingdom
white ensign, Navy

Niue

D
Australia

Anguilla, state

British Virgin
Islands

Cayman Islands

E
Cook Islands

Falkland Islands

Fiji

Montserrat

F
New Zealand

Pitcairn

S. Georgia,
S. Sandwich

St. Helena

G
Tristan da Cunha

Turks and Caicos
Islands

Tuvalu

United Kingdom
blue ensign

H
British Indian
Ocean Territory

1

2

3

4

Band on Hoist Border

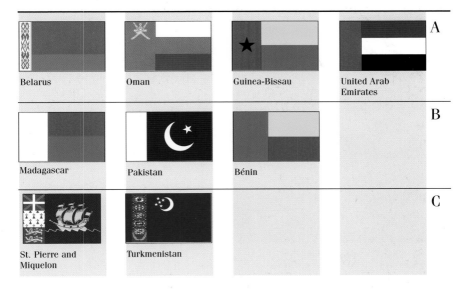

A
- Belarus
- Oman
- Guinea-Bissau
- United Arab Emirates

B
- Madagascar
- Pakistan
- Bénin

C
- St. Pierre and Miquelon
- Turkmenistan

Square or Oblong on Upper Hoist

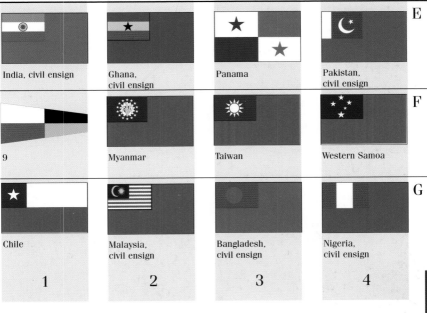

E
- India, civil ensign
- Ghana, civil ensign
- Panama
- Pakistan, civil ensign

F
- 9
- Myanmar
- Taiwan
- Western Samoa

G
- Chile
- Malaysia, civil ensign
- Bangladesh, civil ensign
- Nigeria, civil ensign

1   2   3   4

Circle, Heraldic Creature, X, Diamond

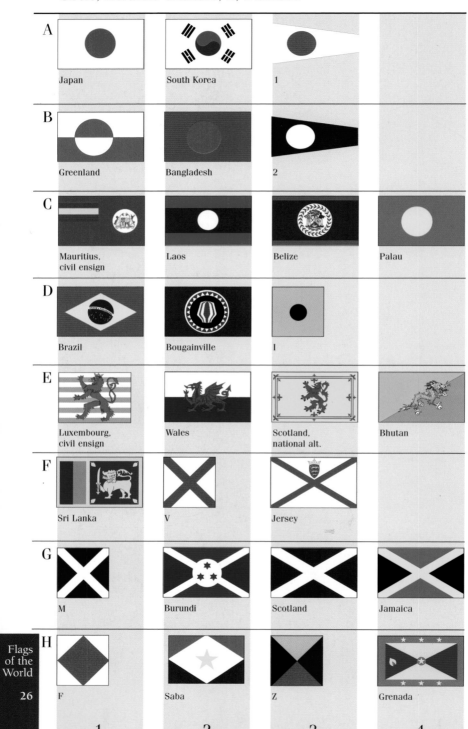

	1	2	3	4
A	Japan	South Korea	1	
B	Greenland	Bangladesh	2	
C	Mauritius, civil ensign	Laos	Belize	Palau
D	Brazil	Bougainville	I	
E	Luxembourg, civil ensign	Wales	Scotland, national alt.	Bhutan
F	Sri Lanka	V	Jersey	
G	M	Burundi	Scotland	Jamaica
H	F	Saba	Z	Grenada

Flags
of the
World

26

Predominant Colour (Red)

B	Switzerland		A
Bahrain	Hong Kong	Qatar	B
Tonga	Tunisia	Turkey	C
China	Macedonia	Kyrgyzstan	Vietnam	D
Montenegro	Albania	Morocco		E
Isle of Man	Wallis and Fortuna	Maldives		F
Nepal				G

| 1 | 2 | 3 | 4 |

Predominant Colour (White)

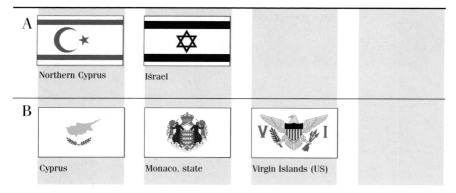

A   Northern Cyprus   Israel

B   Cyprus   Monaco, state   Virgin Islands (US)

Predominant Colour (Yellow)

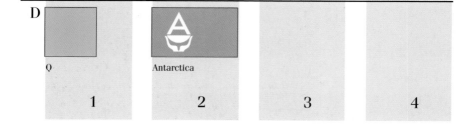

D   Q   Antarctica

1   2   3   4

Predominant Colour (Blue)

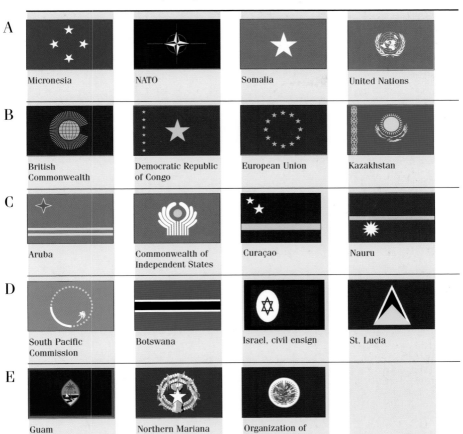

A	Micronesia	NATO	Somalia	United Nations
B	British Commonwealth	Democratic Republic of Congo	European Union	Kazakhstan
C	Aruba	Commonwealth of Independent States	Curaçao	Nauru
D	South Pacific Commission	Botswana	Israel, civil ensign	St. Lucia
E	Guam	Northern Mariana Islands	Organization of American States	

Predominant Colour (Green)

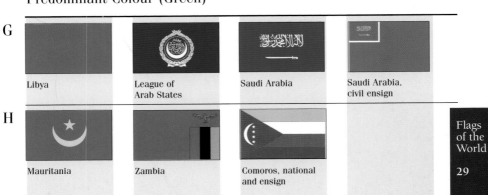

G	Libya	League of Arab States	Saudi Arabia	Saudi Arabia, civil ensign
H	Mauritania	Zambia	Comoros, national and ensign	

1   2   3   4

A • Alpha
- I have a diver down, keep well clear.

B • Bravo
- Taking on, carrying or discharging dangerous cargo.

C • Charlie
- Yes.
- Affirmative.

D • Delta
- I am manoeuvring with difficulty, keep well clear.

E • Echo
- I am altering course to starboard.

F • Foxtrot
- I am disabled. Communicate with me.

G • Golf
- I require a pilot.
- Fishing vessel. I am hauling nets.

H • Hotel
- I have a pilot on board.

I • India
- I am altering course to port.

J • Juliet
- I am on fire, dangerous cargo, keep well clear.

K • Kilo
- I wish to communicate with you.

L • Lima
- Stop your vessel immediately.

M • Mike
- My vessel is stopped.
  I am making no way through the water.

N • November
- No.
- Negative.

O • Oscar
- Man overboard.

P • Papa
- About to proceed to sea. All persons should report on board.
- Fishing boat at sea. My nets are caught on an obstruction.

Flags
of the
World

Q • Quebec
- Request pratique, clearance, and vessel is healthy.

R • Romeo

S • Sierra
- My engines are running with astern propulsion.

T • Tango
- Pair trawling, keep well clear.

U • Uniform
- You are running into danger.

V • Victor
- I require assistance.

W • Whiskey
- I require medical assistance.

X • X-ray
- Stop carrying out your intentions, and watch out for my signals.

Y • Yankee
- I am dragging my anchor.

Z • Zulu
- I require a tug.
- Fishing vessel. I am shooting nets.

1 • One

6 • Six

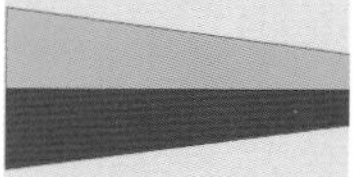

2 • Two

7 • Seven

3 • Three

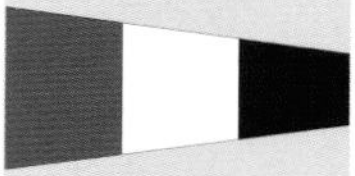

8 • Eight

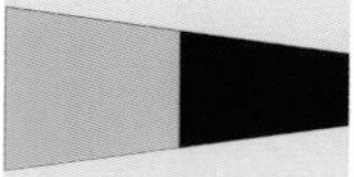

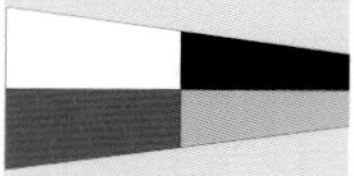

4 • Four

9 • Nine

5 • Five

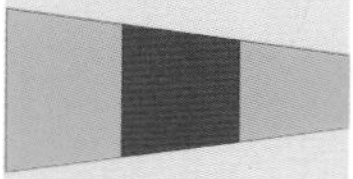

0 • Zero

Repeat Flags

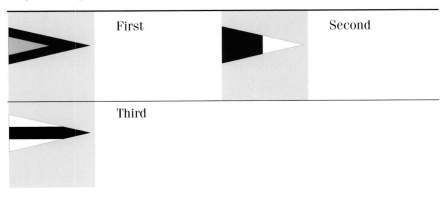

First

Second

Third

Code and Answering Pennant

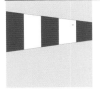

Additional Flag Information

Use of Flags Aboard Ship: Ensigns

SOME FLAGS ARE used almost exclusively at sea and are seldom found on shore. This is true of **ensigns**. Many are identical in design to their national flag; others are similar to, but not exactly like their flag. Occasionally there is no obvious connection between the state flag and the ensign.

SAME FLAGS:
St. Vincent

SIMILAR FLAGS:
Bahamas
Bahamas (civil ensign)

UNALIKE FLAGS:
Luxembourg
Luxembourg (civil ensign)

All ships must fly the ensign of their country of **registry** (usually from the stern). This may not be the same as the country of ownership. There are reasons—often financial—for this apparent discrepancy, and in these cases the ensign shown is known as a flag of convenience. As a vessel enters

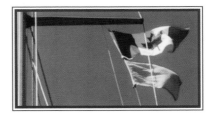

foreign waters, it will also fly a **courtesy** flag, which is a smaller size than its own ensign and is flown from a **spreader** rather than the astern. If the crew happen to be of a nationality different from the registered country, they may fly their own ensign, usually from the port spreader. In the photograph above, a Canadian is on board. The Canadian crew flag with Q code further advises customs that not all aboard are the same nationality as the vessel's registry.

Ensigns may be flown upside down as a signal of distress, but this poses several problems. Many flags are exactly the same either way up—Japan and Jamaica, for instance. Others are difficult to recognize from a distance—which way up is a wildly flapping maple leaf? Other flags have mirror images—how can you distinguish a Polish yacht under perfect control from an Indonesian ship in serious trouble?

Right Way Up Flags:

Inverted Flags:

Similar Flags: Poland & Indonesia

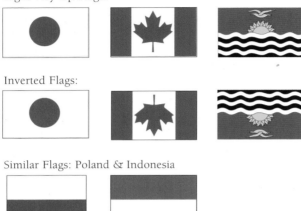

International Code of Signals

FORTUNATELY, THERE IS a far more reliable way of announcing difficulty on board: the alphabetical and numerical flags and pennants that make up the **International Code of Signals** (see pp. 30-34). They have a long history of use at sea. Alone or in groups, they are used all over the world to transmit messages between vessels no matter the native language of the crews. A Greek trawler in mid-ocean can request medical assistance from a Japanese freighter and be clearly understood—despite the fact that neither crew knows a word or even a letter of the other's language. The first signal flown might be the letters MAA—"I request urgent medical advice."

Most of the letters have a distinct meaning, even when flown alone. If you are aboard a cruise ship, at least two will be of interest:

The letter P signals immediate departure. Passengers ashore should hurry back on board, and visitors should leave.

The ship will fly the letter Q as it enters foreign waters, requesting clearance before going ashore.

You will notice that the flags in the International Code of Signals are smaller than ensigns. This is necessary since a series of them may be hoisted to transmit a message. Their ratio is slightly shorter than most flags, being 2:3 rather than the common 1:2. Many of these signal flags are exactly the same whether seen from the **obverse** or **reverse** side. Asymmetrical ones are so characteristic in design that they are unlike any other letter or number. There should be no confusion even if an entire message must be read from the reverse side.

As it is essential to have quick and accurate access to these particular flags, they are usually stowed aboard in a cabinet with small pigeonholes, one for each rolled-up flag. An alternate method of storage is a canvas roll with stitched pockets. The one shown here, hung up for display, is from the 1940s. It was used for an earlier flag signal system.

Canvas roll for signal flags, made by Derek Harrison for the National Maritime Museum, Halifax

Significance of Colours

IN THE CONTEXT of flags, the word "**colours**" has two distinct meanings. It may refer to the entire flag, usually one that belongs to a military unit (like a particular regiment referred to in the order to "strike colours"). The second interpretation is more common, and refers to pigmentation (green is the colour of grass).

There are seven traditional heraldic colours: gold and silver (the **metallic colours**), as well as red, blue, green, black, and purple. Even today the range of colours is quite limited. Each colour can, but does not necessarily, carry specific meaning.

Gold, yellow
Yellow may bear the message of wealth, or a warning of illness. Usually a strong bright yellow is used in modern flags. The richness of metallic gold thread or leaf can be appreciated by examining medieval banners.

Silver, white
Any white cloth or rag, waved or attached to a stick, will be taken as a sign of surrender.

Red
Red may represent martyrdom, danger, revolution, or defiance. It may represent the courage of the people. Generally, vermillion—a bright blood red—is used. There are darker variations such as maroon. Pink is not used.

Blue
Blue has a sense of peacefulness, or it may represent waters important to a country. The flag of the United Nations uses blue in the first sense, Norway in the second.

Green
Associated with safety, youthfulness, and hope, green is also the colour of Islam. There is some variation to this colour, ranging in tinge from yellowish to bluish.

Black
Black can have a very positive meaning, such as pride in the people of a nation. It may, on the other hand, be full of foreboding, death, defiance and anarchy.

Purple
Rarely incorporated in modern flags. It may be used in connection with royalty or high rank.

If you look at a large collection of national flags, you will probably notice that red is predominant. Here is a summary of the percentage of all the flags depicted which incorporate each colour.

| Red: 68% | White: 67% | Blue: 50% | Yellow: 38% |
| Green: 31% | Black: 14% | | |

Flag Families

FLAGS OF SOME NATIONS can be put into groups known as families. This happens when several countries, usually situated fairly close to one another, have chosen the same combination of colours for their flags. Two such groups are shown here as examples. Note that these families do not hold a monopoly on their particular choice of colours. There may be flags of similar colours from countries that are far removed and unrelated.

Pan African Family:

Guyana

Burkina Faso

Togo

Red, yellow, green, and black, though some countries use only three of the colours. Countries in this family are: Benin, Burkina Faso, Cameroon, Central African Republic, Congo, Eritrea, Ethiopia, Ghana, Grenada, Guinea, Guinea-Bissau, Guyana, Mali, Mozambique, São Tome and Príncipe, Senegal, and Togo.

Pan Arab Family:

United Arab Emirates

Kuwait

Egypt

Yemen

The characteristic colours used in this group are red, white, green and black. Some countries use all four, others only three colours. You can see the remarkably close relationship in the flags of Egypt and Yemen.

Glossary

Answering pennant	Flown at the dip (lower) position when a signal has been noticed; it is run up once the message has been received and decoded. It is used with numerical flags as a decimal point between numbers.
Banner	A type of flag usually associated with royal or military use.
Barque	Square-rigged ship with three or more masts. Square sails on all but the last mast, which has fore and aft sails only.
Bunting	Fine wool with a fairly open weave, used for flags.
Burgee	A small flag, often triangular, identifying sailing associations, clubs, or individuals.
Canton (true)	All or part of the top hoist quarter of a flag.
Civil	Applies to flag used by private citizens of a given country.
Colours	Military flags, belonging to a particular unit or regiment.
Courtesy flag	The ensign of a country that a vessel is visiting. Smaller than the ship's ensign and never flown astern.
Defacement	A small symbol, usually on a solid field.
Distal	The edge of a flag away from and opposite the sleeve.
Downhaul	In this context, the end of the flag halyard that is attached to the lower hoist corner of a flag, used to run it downwards.
Ensign	Flag used by vessels to proclaim their country of registry. This may or may not be the same as the national flag of that country.
Flag of Convenience	Vessel registered in, and flies the ensign of, a country which may not be the same as the country of ownership.
Fly	The distal edge of a flag. Subject to much wear as it flies.
Grommet	A metal ring sewn into the sleeve of a flag at its top and lower end for the attachment of a halyard.
Halyard	A continuous line used to hoist a flag to the top of its pole, or to lower it down.
Hoist	That edge of a flag nearest to the staff or halyard.
International Code of Signals	There have been several such codes, revised from time to time. The one now in worldwide use was designed and agreed upon in 1932.
Jack	The flag at the bow of a vessel.

Jack staff	A short perpendicular staff from which the jack flag is flown.
Laid up	As applied to a flag or banner, retired from service to a place of honour.
Length	Measurement along the lower edge of a flag.
Metallic colours	Gold and silver.
Obverse	The side of a flag that faces you when the left border of the flag is attached to the staff, and it is flying freely to the right.
Pennant	A triangular flag with a short hoist tapering to a point at the fly.
Port	The left hand side of a vessel as seen when aboard and facing forward. May be identified at night by a red light.
Pratique	When a vessel comes in to a foreign port, the code flag Q will be flown to request certification of a clean bill of health. Until this is granted, the vessel and personnel are in quarantine. When pratique is granted, the Q flag will be lowered, and crew may go ashore.
Ratio	Relation of width to length of a flag. This varies, but most flags are 1:2.
Registry	The country in which a vessel is registered.
Repeat flag	Substitute or repeat flags. If only one set of flags is available these flags allow a letter that occurs more than once in a word to be repeated.
Retired	See **Laid up**.
Reverse	The side of a flag opposite to the obverse.
Sleeve	A tube of strong fabric sewn along the hoist of a flag. A line may be run through the sleeve to be attached to the halyard.
Staff	A short flag pole.
Standard	A flag of royalty or nobility, often quite ornate. When flown from a castle or palace, it signifies that the owner is in residence.
Starboard	The right hand side of a vessel as seen when aboard, facing forward. Identified by a green light at night.
State flag	One used by the government.
Vexilloid	Forerunner of modern flags. A staff with a carved symbolic image, used in ancient Roman times.
Vexillology	The study of flags.
Width	The measurement of a flag from top to lower edge.

Answer Page

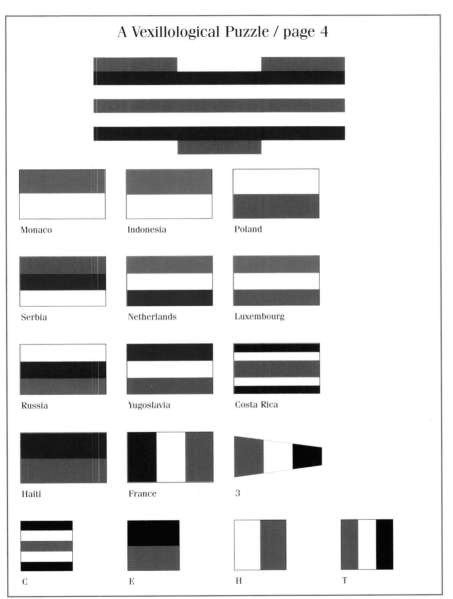

A Vexillological Puzzle / page 4

Monaco

Indonesia

Poland

Serbia

Netherlands

Luxembourg

Russia

Yugoslavia

Costa Rica

Haiti

France

3

C

E

H

T

Answer to the flag identification / page 10

Top: (Left) Vatican City; (Right) Croatia
Middle, from top to bottom: LXSF. Flying aboard the Luxembourg registered
sailing ship *Star Flyer*.
Bottom: (Left) Germany; (Right) Madeira

Bibliography

Collier, Captain J. R. *Yachting Signal Book*. Centreville: Cornell Maritime Press, 1985.

Crampton, William. *DK Eyewitness Guides: Flag*. London: Dorling Kindersley, 1989.

Crampton, William. *Spotter's Guide to Flags of the World*. London: UE Usborne House, 2003.

Evans, I. O. *The Observer's Book of Flags*. London: Frederick Warne, 1959.

Heady, Sue. *Pocket Guide to Flags*. London: PRC Publishing, 2001.

Heritage Canada. *Flag Etiquette in Canada*. Ottawa: Minister of Supply and Services, 2001.

Hewitt, Commander R. L. and the Royal Yachting Association. *Flag Etiquette & Visual Signals*. Hampshire: RYA House, 2001.

Johnson, Peter. *Reed's Maritime Flags*. Wiltshire: Thomas Reed Publications, 2002.

Russell, Captain P. J. *Sea Signalling Simplified*. London: Adlard Coles, 1969.

Shaw, Carol P. *Collins Gem Flags*. Glasgow: Harper Collins Publishers, 1999.

Smith, Whitney. *Flag Lore of All Nations*. Brookfield: Millbrook Press, 2001.

Transport Canada. *International Code of Signals*. Ottawa: Canada Communications Group, 1994.

Znamierowski, Alfred. *Flags of the World*. London: Southwater, Anness Publishing, 2000.

Znamierowski, Alfred. *World Flags Identifier*. London: Lorenz Books, Anness Publishing, 2001.

Znamierowski, Alfred. *The World Encyclopaedia of Flags*. London: Anness Publishing, 2001.

Index

H

I

J

K

L